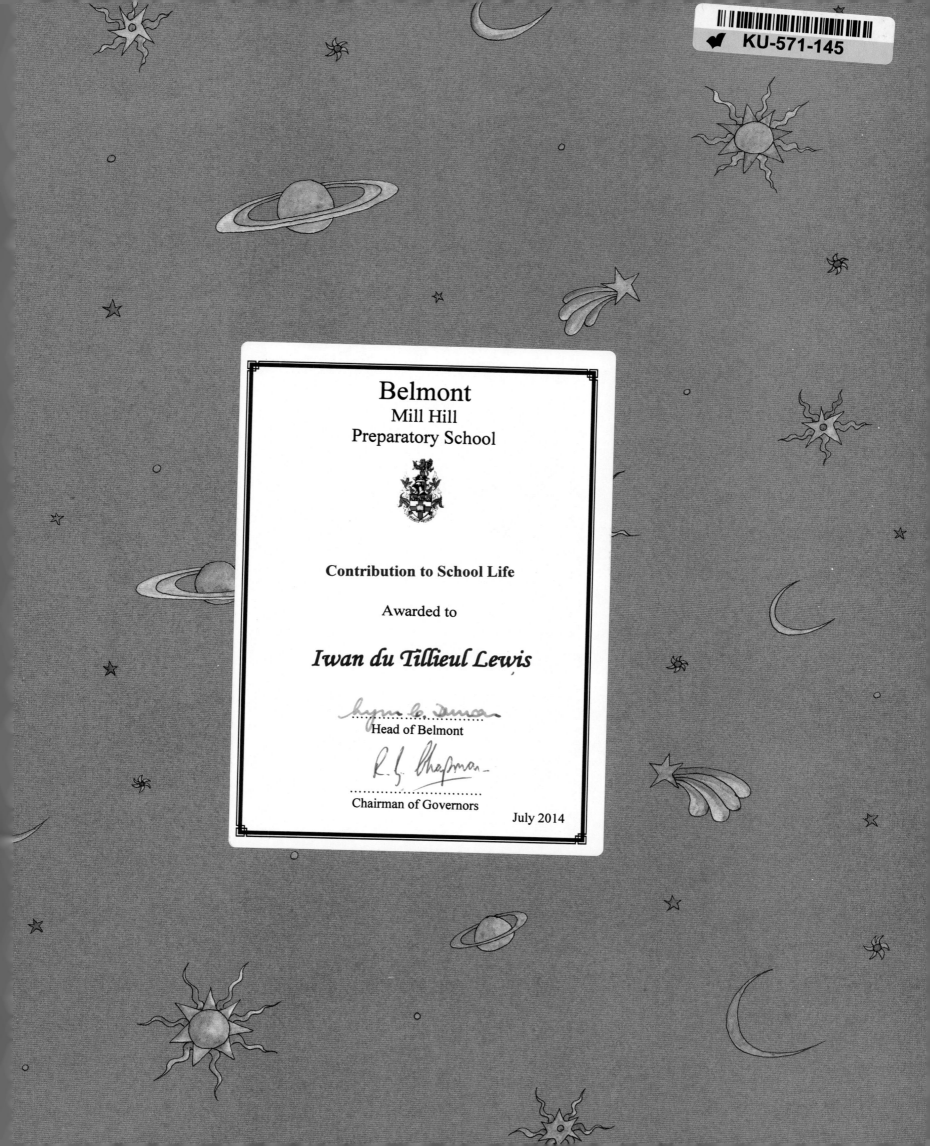

Belmont
Mill Hill
Preparatory School

Contribution to School Life

Awarded to

Iwan du Tillieul Lewis

Head of Belmont

Chairman of Governors

July 2014

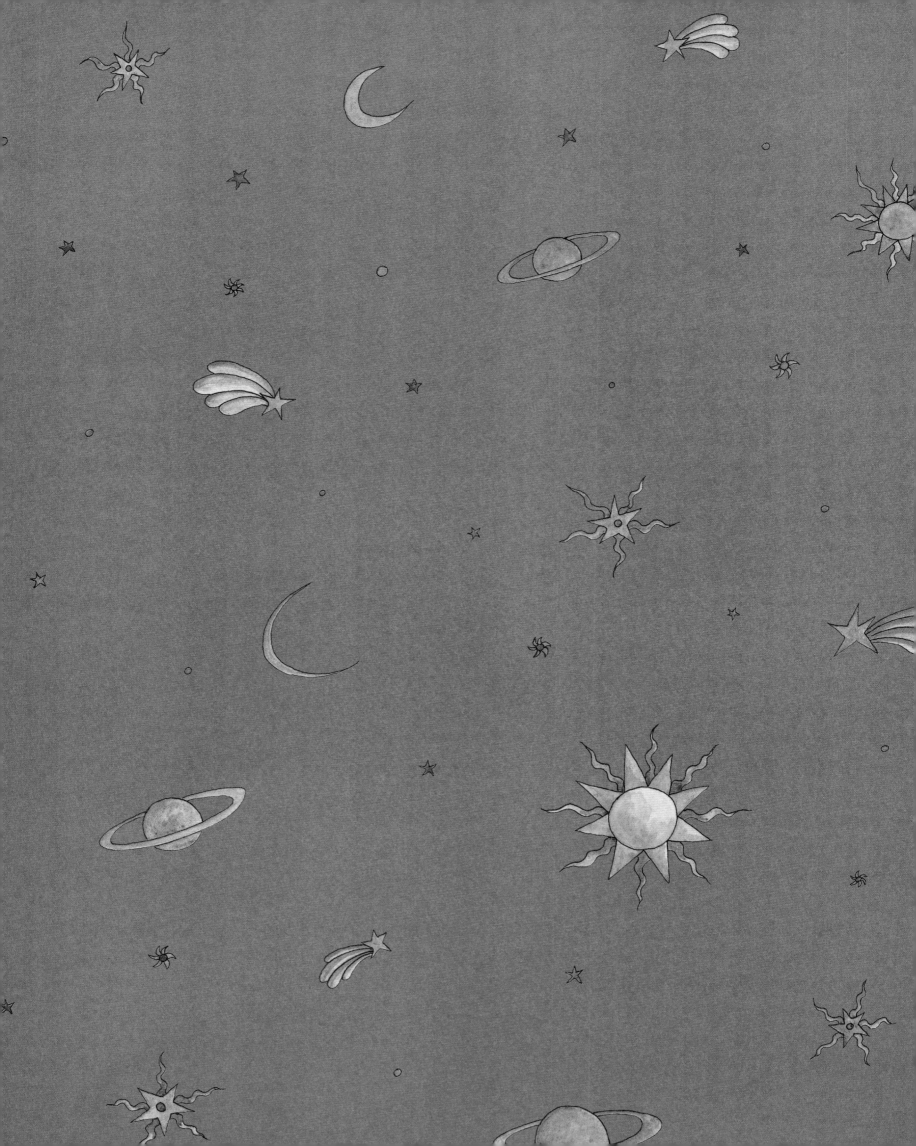

Dear Play-goer

Imagine you have been transported to the England of William Shakespeare's time. On the banks of the River Thames is the Globe Theatre, the wooden building where all the plays in this book are to be performed. See if you can spot Queen Elizabeth I and Shakespeare himself among the spectators.

There are seats at bargain prices! For a penny you can stand in the open courtyard with other "groundlings" and see the play — watch out for pickpockets though! For tuppence you can sit among richer people in one of the covered galleries and for an extra penny you can sit in comfort on a cushion!

There are three parts to each performance: the words that Shakespeare actually wrote are those spoken by the actors; the story, or the plot of the play, is told underneath the pictures; and the spectators — who are famously rude and noisy — can be seen and heard around the stage.

Ladies and gentlemen — take your seats. The performance is about to begin...

The audience is asked to refrain from throwing hard objects at the performers. Rotten fruit and veg only, please!

First published individually as *Mr. William Shakespeare's Plays* (1998) and *Bravo, Mr. William Shakespeare!* (2000)
by Walker Books Ltd, 87 Vauxhall Walk, London SE11 5HJ

This edition published 2014

2 4 6 8 10 9 7 5 3 1

© 1998, 2000 Marcia Williams

The right of Marcia Williams to be identified as author/illustrator of this work
has been asserted by her in accordance with the Copyright, Designs and Patents Act 1988

This book has been typeset in Monotype Centaur and Truesdell

Printed in China

British Library Cataloguing in Publication Data:
a catalogue record for this book is available from the British Library

ISBN 978-1-4063-5760-8

www.walker.co.uk

www.marciawilliams.co.uk

For Jill and Ella

With thanks to Wendy, Helen,
Bridget, Stephanie and Martin

The Marvellous Plays of
Mr William Shakespeare

Presented by
Marcia Williams

WALKER BOOKS
AND SUBSIDIARIES
LONDON • BOSTON • SYDNEY • AUCKLAND

The Globe Theatre
is proud to present a new season of

The Marvellous Plays of

Mr William Shakespeare

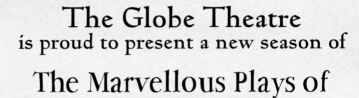

Romeo and Juliet

What will happen when two lovers disobey their feuding families
and follow their hearts? The most famous and tragic love story
of all time! *Page 10*

Hamlet

The young Prince of Denmark struggles with his conscience
as he tries to avenge his murdered father in Will's powerful
and philosophical tragedy. *Page 14*

A Midsummer Night's Dream

Love is not what it seems in this delightful comedy, where
magic leaves fairies and mortals hopelessly entangled. *Page 18*

Macbeth

How far will a man go to become king? Set in the wilds of Scotland,
this is a dark and bloody tale about the evils of ambition. *Page 24*

The Winter's Tale

A tale told across two generations of jealousy, regret
and the redemptive power of love. *Page 30*

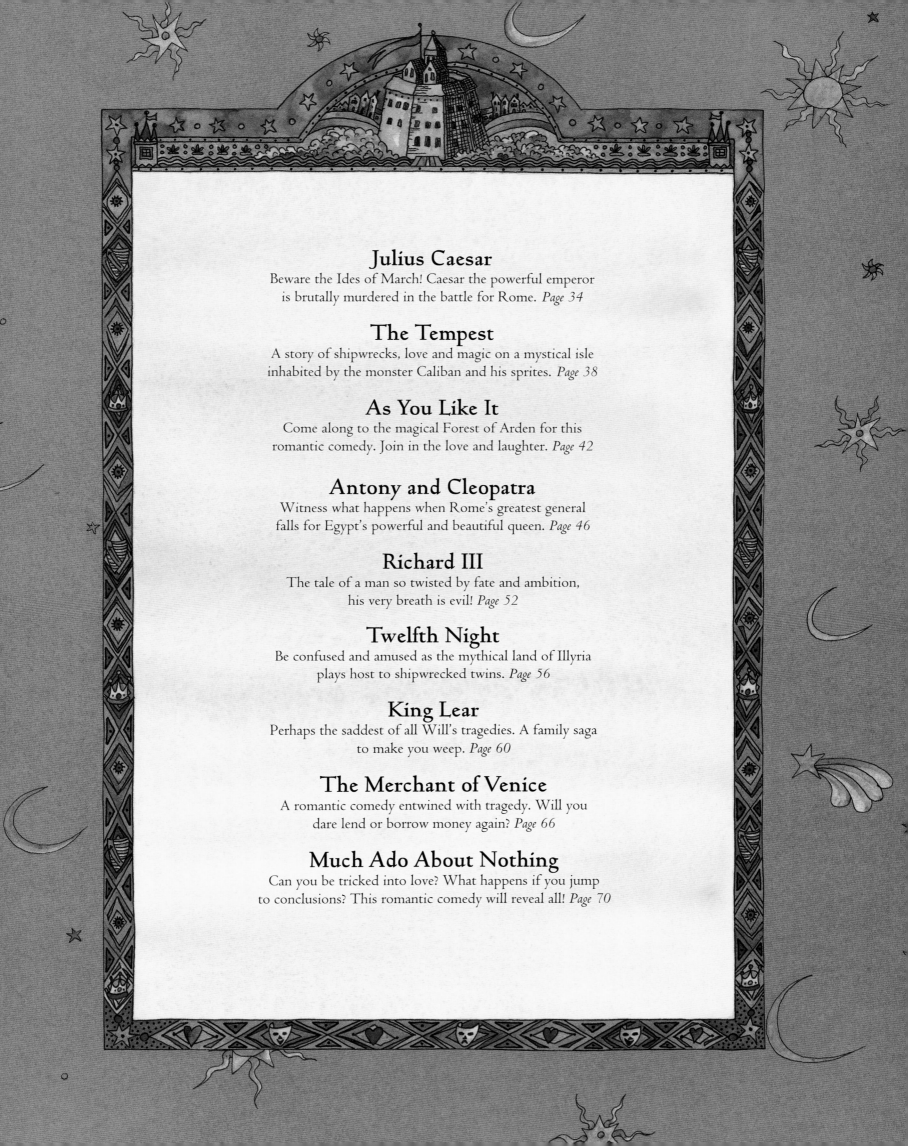

ROMEO and JULIET

MONTAGUES

CAPULETS

*Go, sirrah, trudge about
Through fair Verona; find
those persons out
Whose names are written there,
and to them say,
My house and welcome on
their pleasure stay.*

*I am sent to find those persons
Whose names are here writ...
I must to the learned.*

*Do you bite your
thumb at us, sir?*

In the ancient Italian city of Verona, Lord Capulet was planning a party. He was sure no members of the Montague family would turn up, as the Capulets and Montagues had been feuding for years. The quarrel ran so deep that even their servants fought. But Lord Capulet was wrong.

*Is love a tender thing? It is too rough,
Too rude, too boisterous; and it pricks like thorn.*

*Did my heart love
till now?*

Romeo, Lord Montague's son, and Mercutio, his friend, *did* come — in disguise. He was infatuated with Lord Capulet's niece, Rosaline.

Romeo, however, instantly forgot Rosaline when he saw Lord Capulet's sweet young daughter Juliet. Her beauty stole his heart.

*Uncle, this is
a Montague!*

Young Romeo, is it?

*O! She doth
teach the
torches to burn
bright.*

Nuts
for sale!
Eat my
fine
nuts!

*'Tis a
shame.*

He shall be endur'd.

*A snowy dove
trooping with crows.*

*The only
son of your
great enemy.*

*My only love
sprung
from my
only
hate!*

And
her
only 13.

Unfortunately, Romeo was recognized by Lord Capulet's fiery nephew, Tybalt.

But Lord Capulet forbade fighting at his ball and made Romeo welcome.

So Romeo wooed Juliet and soon their love was mutual, despite the feud.

Will you
be my
Juliet?

No!

He loves her.

Go on!
Kiss her.

As the party ended, Juliet ran to her balcony to declare her love for Romeo to the stars.

Romeo risked death by climbing the Capulets' orchard wall to see Juliet.

That night, the loving pair agreed to wed in secret, lest their feuding families part them.

Buzz off.

As dawn broke and Juliet's nurse finally got her to bed, Romeo raced to Friar Laurence.

The friar agreed to marry the sweethearts, hoping this would unite the families.

Later that morning, Juliet joined Romeo at the chapel, and the happy pair were wed.

Soppy nonsense!

Yes, dear.

Then Romeo and Juliet parted, as they knew they must, until Friar Laurence had broken the news to their families.

On the way home, Romeo met his good friends Benvolio and Mercutio, being harangued by Tybalt for consorting with a Montague.

Watch, dear. Nice Mr Shakespeare wrote this just for you.

Boring.

Romeo, now related to Tybalt by his marriage, tried to prevent a fight, but failed.

Tybalt and Mercutio's swords clashed and Mercutio fell dead.

Provoked by his friend's death, Romeo struck Tybalt a fatal blow.

Well done, boys, nice deaths.

Hey, get that bear off there.

Is he really dead, Mum?

Juliet was carried to the family burial vault, from where, according to the friar's plan, Romeo would rescue her.

But the friar's letter, telling Romeo of the scheme, went astray. A messenger told Romeo the false news of Juliet's sudden "death".

Romeo bought poison and went to the tomb. There he found Paris who, in his misery, attacked Romeo, who slew him in defence.

Then Romeo gave Juliet a kiss and drank the poison. Just too late, Friar Laurence arrived, now aware that his letter had not reached Romeo.

As the friar cried out in horror, Juliet awoke to see Romeo, lifeless beside her.

Hearing voices approach, the friar fled. But Juliet, unable to imagine life without Romeo, took up his dagger and, stabbing herself, fell dead upon her husband's body.

When the families of the Montagues and Capulets arrived upon this tragic scene, they were grief stricken at the consequences of their vendetta. Lord Capulet and Lord Montague vowed to raise a golden statue to each other's child. Thus they buried their feud, along with their precious children, Romeo and his sweet Juliet.

HAMLET
Prince of Denmark

As Hamlet, Prince of Denmark, kept watch with his friend Horatio on the battlements of Elsinore Castle, his father's ghost appeared to him. The dead king told Hamlet that he had been murdered by his brother, Claudius, and urged Hamlet to take revenge.

Gentle Hamlet had idolized his father and was outraged when his mother, Queen Gertrude, married his Uncle Claudius, who then became king. But Hamlet had not suspected his uncle of murder.

Hamlet kept the ghost's secret but all at court, including the king's chamberlain, Polonius, noticed how unstable Hamlet had become.

He often exaggerated his madness, so that his Uncle Claudius and Polonius would not realize that he was suspicious.

Even Ophelia, Polonius' daughter, suffered Hamlet's erratic behaviour. Hamlet's feelings for her fluctuated between tenderness and scorn.

Unable to trust anyone at court, Hamlet felt miserable and confused. Should he take his own life or that of his father's murderer, Claudius?

Thou know'st 'tis common: All that live must die.

I am but mad north-north-west: When the wind is southerly I know a hawk from a handsaw.

Hamlet's mother, unaware that Claudius had murdered Hamlet's father, thought his madness was grief for the good king's death.

Polonius was sure that Hamlet's madness stemmed from his love for Ophelia. Only Claudius feared a more sinister reason.

Good thinking, Hammy!

I'll have these players Play something like the murder of my father Before mine uncle: I'll observe his looks.

Meanwhile Hamlet's distress grew daily as he watched his mother, so recently widowed, and his murderous uncle together. Yet he hesitated to take revenge without more evidence. Then the arrival of an acting troupe gave Hamlet an idea of how to unmask King Claudius.

That Dane has had his bacon!

Thy natural magic and dire property, on wholesome life usurp immediately.

Give me some light: away!

Give o'er the play.

O good Horatio! I'll take the ghost's word for a thousand pound.

You've no excuse now, Hamlet.

Before the assembled court, the actors, on Hamlet's orders, put on a play mimicking the ghost's story of his murder and its consequences. Claudius was so affected by the murder scene that he rushed from the room; Hamlet no longer doubted his uncle's guilt.

He's going to his mother's closet: Behind the arras I'll convey myself.

Thanks.

Hamlet, thou hast thy father much offended.

Mother, you have my father much offended.

Come, come, you answer with an idle tongue.

Go, go, you question with a wicked tongue.

Help, help, ho!

What, ho! Help, help, help!

Hot-blooded, Danes.

Claudius realized that he had been discovered and, hoping to learn more, encouraged Polonius to spy on Hamlet and Queen Gertrude.

From behind the drapes, Polonius overheard Hamlet grow violent when his mother spoke of Claudius as his "father". He cried out in alarm.

'Ere, I'm the rat-catcher around here.

How now! A rat? Dead, for a ducat, dead!

O! I am slain.

O me! What hast thou done?

Do you not come your tardy son to chide?

Do not forget!

Alas! He's mad.

He hasn't got the bottle.

Hamlet, thinking it was Claudius' voice, plunged his sword through the drapes, killing Polonius. Anger made Hamlet unrepentant.

Hamlet continued to chide his mother until his father's ghost appeared, urging him to be gentler, but to avenge his death.

No, but you have!

Get that vermin out.

That ghost is asking too much.

I'm sick of standing.

Lovely oranges!

I think that poor Hamlet'll top himself.

Polonius' death gave Claudius an excuse to be rid of Hamlet. Claudius sent the Prince to England with two of his spies, who carried a letter ordering the English to execute Hamlet upon arrival. But Hamlet found the letter and exchanged the spies' names for his own.

On the journey, their ship was attacked by pirates. Hamlet leapt aboard to fight, while his companions fled to England – and their deaths.

The pirates, discovering that they had Prince Hamlet on board, returned him safely to Denmark, hoping for future favours.

At Elsinore, Hamlet was greeted with the news of Ophelia's death. Deranged by her father's violent end, Ophelia had been garlanding a willow tree when she fell into the brook below and drowned. Hamlet was heartbroken. So too was Laertes, who mourned her loss as only a brother can.

In fact, Laertes blamed Hamlet for killing both his father and his sister and he longed for Hamlet's death as much as Claudius did. The pair therefore plotted to kill Hamlet and make his death look like an accident. To this end they issued a challenge to the Prince.

Hamlet was tempted into a fencing match with Laertes, who fought with a poisoned sword instead of a blunt foil. When Laertes drew blood, Hamlet let fly his fury and, in the scuffle, the swords changed hands. Then Laertes too was wounded by his own deadly weapon.

That same night six Athenian workmen went to the wood, to rehearse in secret a play for Duke Theseus' wedding to Hippolyta.

Nearby the fairy king, Oberon, with his sprite Puck, was arguing with Queen Titania over a changeling boy they both wanted.

Oberon, annoyed, planned a trick: he sent Puck to fetch a plant, whose juice made people love the first creature they saw upon waking.

Now, as it happened, Demetrius, with Helena in hot pursuit, passed close to Oberon's hiding place.

Pitying love-sick Helena, Oberon, on Puck's return, told him to anoint Demetrius' eyelids, thinking he would wake to see Helena.

Meanwhile, Oberon found his sleeping queen, Titania. He squeezed the flower's magic juice upon her eyelids.

But Puck mistook Lysander, sleeping near Hermia, for Demetrius and anointed his eyes with the flower's juice.

Then, as luck would have it, Helena, still in pursuit of Demetrius, tripped over Lysander in the dark and woke him!

Not Hermia, but Helena I love.

Do not say so.

So, by the flower's magic, Lysander forgot his love for Hermia and fell instantly in love with Helena.

To honour Helen, and to be her knight!

Wherefore was I to this keen mockery born?

Shocked by Lysander's unexpected love, Helena ran off, pursued by Lysander.

I swoon almost with fear.

Thus, poor Hermia woke alone. Fearfully, she set out in search of Lysander.

Which is the proper play?

Are we all met?

Pat, pat; and here's a marvellous convenient place for our rehearsal.

All this while Titania slept on, unaware that the troupe of Athenians, led by Bottom and Peter Quince, had chosen to rehearse their play nearby. It was a perfect opportunity for the mischievous Puck to play one of his tricks, for Titania's eyelids still glistened with magic juice.

If I were, fair Thisby, I were only thine.

Yoo-hoo Puck.

Has he got fleas?

Suddenly, at the height of the action, Bottom the weaver appeared wearing an ass's head! The other actors fled in fright. Then Puck, who had transformed Bottom into this ridiculous creature, guided him to the sleeping Titania's side.

Get her jewels next.

Sssh! I'm listening.

How do they do that?

Can we do that to daddy?

I need to wee!

When Titania awoke, the first creature she saw was Bottom with an ass's head! Instantly, she fell in love with him. Bottom was not displeased by the attention, especially when Titania ordered her fairies to attend his every whim.

As Puck reported all this to Oberon, Hermia hurried past. Demetrius was close behind but now, exhausted and disheartened, he paused to rest. Realizing Puck's error, Oberon sent him to fetch Helena while he anointed Demetrius' lids with the flower juice.

In my day, love was so simple.

At last, a fight!

So when Demetrius awoke and saw Helena, he loved her once again. Helena, far from being happy about this, believed herself mocked.

When Hermia arrived she quickly understood that both Lysander *and* Demetrius now loved Helena. Hermia screamed abuse at Helena.

I'm blowed if I know what's going on.

Fancy a grown man writing about fairies.

Puck, on Oberon's orders, drew the lovers on and on until, tired and confused, they fell asleep.

Then Puck anointed Lysander's eyelids in order to restore his love for Hermia.

As Bottom lay sleeping in Titania's arms, Oberon put an antidote on her lids.

Disgusting! Kissing, yuk!

Are the fairies on strings?

Then Oberon woke Titania, who was so mortified at being seen with a snoring ass that she promised Oberon the changeling boy.

Oberon, satisfied at last, danced happily away with Titania, leaving Puck to restore Bottom to his usual self.

Does your cat like Shakespeare?

I look stupid!

Just think what might happen if you got fairy dust up your nostrils.

He's been translated again!

My love shall hear the music of my hounds.

I beg the law!

As day dawned, a hunting party entered the woods, led by Duke Theseus and Hippolyta; Egeus was also in the party.

When they happened upon the reunited lovers, Egeus was still eager to impose the law of Athens on his daughter, Hermia.

Well roared, lion.

Well shone, moon.

ROAR!

O sweet and lovely wall. Show me thy chink.

Are we the audience or are they?

Did you pay for two plays?

RESERVED

But it was Theseus' wedding day and when he saw the young people back with their original loved ones, he over-ruled Egeus. He bade the party return to Athens and resolved to have all three couples wed that very day: himself to Hippolyta, Hermia to Lysander and Helena to Demetrius. After the ceremony, Bottom and his troupe were called to put on their play, which earned them all a goodly sum and much applause. Then the whole company, at last restored to happy harmony, retired to bed.

Hand in hand, with fairy grace, Will we sing, and bless this place.

IF WE SHADOWS HAVE OFFENDED, THINK BUT THIS, AND ALL IS MENDED. THAT YOU HAVE BUT SLUMBER'D HERE, WHILE THESE VISIONS DID APPEAR.

Ooh! That's so pretty.

Slumber, with all that going on?

That left the way clear for the fairy king and queen, attended by Puck, to bless the palace of Theseus and bid all goodnight – the perfect end to the story, or to a beautifully woven midsummer night's dream in an enchanted wood.

SOLD OUT

Are they all happy now?

We've got fairies in our house!

Most people call them fleas!

Well that's what I call a finale!

MACBETH

Macbeth and Banquo, two Scottish generals living under the reign of King Duncan, were returning home to Inverness across a bleak heath. They had just bravely defeated an army of rebels much to the delight of the king, who was also Macbeth's cousin.

Suddenly, as if from nowhere, three hideous witches appeared. The first witch greeted Macbeth as Thane (or Lord) of Glamis, which was his correct title. The second greeted him as Thane of Cawdor, which was not, and the third as King of Scotland, an honour held by Duncan.

Just before the witches vanished they also prophesied that Banquo would never be king, but that he would father kings.

As the two generals stood, stunned, news arrived that the king had made Macbeth Thane of Cawdor, in honour of his victory.

Death-knell music.
Don't pick your nose, the Queen's here.
Three mugs to crack one nut!
Talking of nuts, your honour.

Their hands and faces were all badg'd with blood.
O! Yet I do repent me of my fury, That I did kill them.

With their daggers bloodied, the grooms were blamed. Macbeth, claiming vengeance, killed them both to safeguard his secret.

Help me hence, ho!
I'll to England.
To Ireland, I.

Despite their display of grief, many suspected the Macbeths of the murder. The king's sons, fearing for their own lives, fled Scotland.

Thou hast it now: King, Cawdor, Glamis, all.

Macbeth, as next in line to the throne, was then crowned king, fulfilling the third prophecy.

To be thus is nothing; But to be safely thus: Our fears in Banquo stick deep.

Haunted by guilt, but still anxious to retain power, Macbeth worried that Banquo's descendants, not his own, would one day reign as had also been foretold.

O, treachery! Fly, good Fleance, fly, fly, fly! Thou mayst revenge.

So Macbeth resolved to murder Banquo and his son, Fleance, and to this end invited all the local thanes to a feast. As Banquo and Fleance made their way to the palace, they were brutally attacked by Macbeth's hired assassins. Fleance managed to escape, but Banquo died.

Thou canst not say I did it: never shake Thy gory locks at me.

Oblivious to this horrific deed, the other thanes were merrily dining when Banquo's ghost suddenly appeared. Only Macbeth could see the spectre and it so unnerved him that the Queen dismissed their guests, lest they wonder at the strange behaviour of their king.

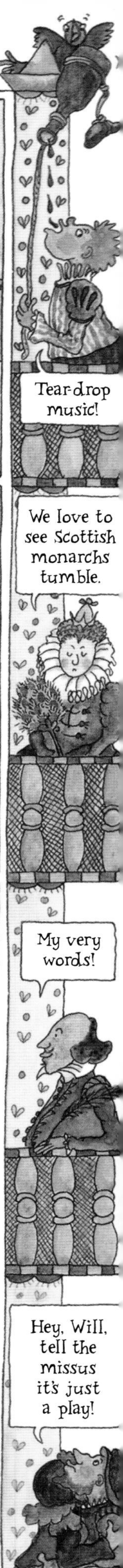
Tear-drop music!
We love to see Scottish monarchs tumble.
My very words!
Hey, Will, tell the missus it's just a play!

Didn't I see you at Hamlet?
Sure, I never miss a gloomy one!
Eggs for sale!

Thereafter Macbeth and his queen began to suffer long, sleepless nights, filled with hideous dreams. Yet Macbeth was still obsessed with not losing the throne, so he returned to the heath to seek out the witches. He found them in a cave, chanting over a cauldron of boiling hell-broth from which three apparitions rose: the first was an armed head, which warned Macbeth to beware of Macduff, the Thane of Fife; the second was a bloody child, who told Macbeth that no man born of woman could harm him; the third was another child, wearing a crown and holding a tree, who reassured Macbeth that he would never be vanquished until Great Birnam Wood came to Dunsinane Hill, where Macbeth's castle stood.

When Macbeth asked if Banquo's heirs would reign, the cauldron sank into the ground and eight ghostly kings passed by, followed by Banquo's ghost. The last king carried a glass which showed many kings, and Macbeth knew them to be Banquo's descendants.

From this day, insecurity plagued Macbeth. So when he heard that Macduff, Thane of Fife, had joined forces with Prince Malcolm, Macbeth ordered the death of Macduff's wife and children. This bloody deed lost Macbeth many friends and determined Malcolm and Macduff to seek revenge.

Then Macbeth received a terrible blow: his queen, who had never come to terms with her guilt and whose nights and days were ceaselessly haunted by ghastly visions, finally succumbed to death. Macbeth felt totally alone. Still more grave news followed…

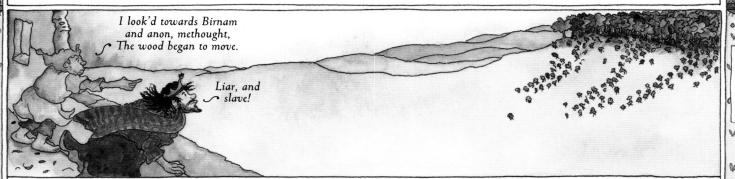

Thousands of Prince Malcolm's troops were fast approaching, shielded behind branches cut from Great Birnam Wood. Thus it appeared that the wood moved towards Dunsinane Hill and Macbeth's castle, the event predicted to precede Macbeth's downfall.

Macbeth still believed himself invulnerable. Rallying his remaining forces, he waged a bloody war until he met Macduff, face to face. When Macduff disclosed that he had not been born by natural means, but by Caesarean birth with the help of a surgeon, Macbeth knew his end had come.

Now, Prince Malcolm, the rightful heir, claimed his father's throne. Macbeth was dead and the people rejoiced. The wicked reign of Macbeth and his ambitious queen had ended just as had been prophesied. Scotland was at peace, ruled once more by a true and noble king.

The Winter's Tale

> What a cosy scene.

> Stay your thanks awhile, And pay them when you part.

> Sir, that's tomorrow.

> Aaah! He's going to lose his best friend.

One winter, King Leontes of Sicily, Queen Hermione and their young son, Mamillius, were contentedly awaiting the birth of a second child. Polixenes, King of Bohemia, had come to visit and was now about to depart, much against Leontes' wishes.

> Aah! Poli, what a chum.

> Is he won yet?

> He'll stay, my lord.

But Hermione succeeded where her husband had failed, and persuaded Polixenes to stay longer with them.

> My heart dances; but not for joy.

> He something seems unsettled.

> Ooh! The little green-eyed monster!

Instead of pleasing Leontes, this made him insanely jealous. He thought that Hermione and Polixenes must be in love.

> Rotten toms to throw!

> My wife is slippery?

> Be cur'd of this diseas'd opinion.

King Leontes told Camillo, his advisor, of his belief, wishing him to poison Polixenes.

> My favour here begins to warp.

> Come, sir, away!

Unable to change Leontes' mind, Camillo fled with Polixenes to Bohemia.

> A sad tale's best for winter.

> Can I hear it too?

Meanwhile, Mamillius related a sad tale to distract his mother from the king's anger.

> Hey, give us a tom to splodge on his jealous nose!

> Well, I believe Leontes.

> Nuts!

> Why am I a stinkard?

> 'Cos you pong, dearie!

I'm glad he's not my dad!

Bear the boy hence; he shall not come about her... Away with her to prison!

Beseech your highness call the queen again.

Be certain what you do, sir, lest your justice prove violence.

Hold your peaces!

Ooh! He's such a tyrant!

Camillo and Polixenes' escape increased Leontes' fury and he imprisoned Hermione. Little Mamillius was heartbroken and refused to eat.

King Leontes was unrepentant. Hoping to prove his wife's guilt, he sent two lords to consult the Oracle at Delphi, in Greece.

Where's your heart?

The good queen, For she is good, hath brought you forth a daughter: Here 'tis; commends it to your blessing.

Out! A mankind witch!

Take it up. I'll not rear another's issue.

Come on, poor babe.

We are glad we never married.

In prison, Hermione gave birth to a daughter, Perdita. Her friend Paulina, in a bid to soften Leontes' heart, took the baby to the king.

Leontes was unmoved. Believing Polixenes to be the baby's father, he ordered that Perdita be abandoned on some foreign shore.

Is that the end?

HERMIONE IS CHASTE;
POLIXENES BLAMELESS;
CAMILLO A TRUE SUBJECT;
LEONTES A JEALOUS TYRANT;
HIS INNOCENT BABE TRULY BEGOTTEN;
AND THE KING SHALL LIVE WITHOUT
AN HEIR IF THAT WHICH IS LOST BE
NOT FOUND.

There is no truth at all i' the oracle: the sessions shall proceed.

Apollo's angry.

This news is mortal to the queen.

Angry. He must be livid!

As the wrongly accused queen stood trial, the messengers returned from Delphi. The Oracle proclaimed Hermione innocent!

Leontes declared the Oracle false and bid the trial continue.

But when news came of Mamillius' death, Hermione collapsed.

Hey, that Apollo chappy won't pardon you.

Apollo, pardon.

Woe the while! O cut my lace, lest my heart cracking it, break too.

Will you swear never to marry but by my free leave?

Never, Paulina: so be my blessed spirit.

Who'd have you anyway?

Paulina took her from the court and at last Leontes repented of his mad jealousy.

But it seemed he repented too late, for Paulina returned to say that Hermione had died.

King Leontes was desolate. He swore never to remarry and to live a life of mourning.

You don't deserve no pardon.

Put a plum in it.

Meanwhile, a storm drove the ship carrying Perdita on to the shores of Bohemia. Perdita, with a bundle of keepsakes, was saved, but the ship and all its crew were lost.

Luckily, Perdita was found by a shepherd who cared for her as a daughter for fifteen years.

Perdita was so delightful that Prince Florizel, son of King Polixenes, fell in love with her.

All this time, Camillo was also in Bohemia but unaware of Perdita. Polixenes was angry that his son was courting a shepherdess and asked Camillo to visit her.

Well disguised, Polixenes and Camillo met Florizel and Perdita and were innocently asked to witness their engagement.

Polixenes suddenly threw off his disguise. He forbade his son to marry a shepherdess and he ordered Florizel to return to court.

But Camillo, charmed by the pair, persuaded them to escape to Sicily and beg King Leontes' help, while he sought Polixenes' approval.

King Leontes welcomed Polixenes' son. Alas, Perdita's striking likeness to Hermione brought sad memories flooding back.

As King Leontes talked of the past, it dawned on the shepherd, who had escorted the pair, that Perdita could be Leontes' daughter. Many rumours flew about as to how this was proven, but it *was* proven and the king was beside himself with happiness.

Leontes took his daughter to see a statue of her mother Hermione, rumoured to be kept by Paulina. In spite of the welcome arrival of Polixenes and Camillo, Leontes could not take his eyes off the life-like statue.

Then Paulina called for music and, to everyone's amazement, the statue began to move. Hermione descended the pedestal. The time had come for the queen to be reunited with her family and friends.

King Polixenes, discovering his son's shepherdess to be a princess, gave his blessing for Florizel and Perdita's marriage, joining the two families in harmony once more. King Leontes gave Paulina's hand in marriage to Camillo, for they held each other in deep affection. Thus ended the strange story of how Paulina had kept Hermione hidden and how Perdita had been found — a wonderful winter's tale to tell by the fireside.

JULIUS CAESAR

It was a day of celebration and the streets of Ancient Rome swarmed with citizens cheering Julius Caesar's victory over his rival, Pompey. At that time, Rome was a Republic – ruled by the people through their Senators. Now some politicians feared that Caesar would want to rule Rome himself.

As Caesar paraded to the games, a soothsayer warned him to beware the Ides of March, or the fifteenth day of the month. Caesar scoffed.

Two Senators, Brutus and Cassius, watched Caesar's triumphant expression. They supported the Republic, and feared Caesar's ambition.

On his return from the games, Caesar did not look so pleased. Casca, a friend of the two Senators, explained what had happened:

Caesar's supporter, Mark Antony, had offered him the crown. Caesar refused it, but to his dismay, the crowd roared its approval!

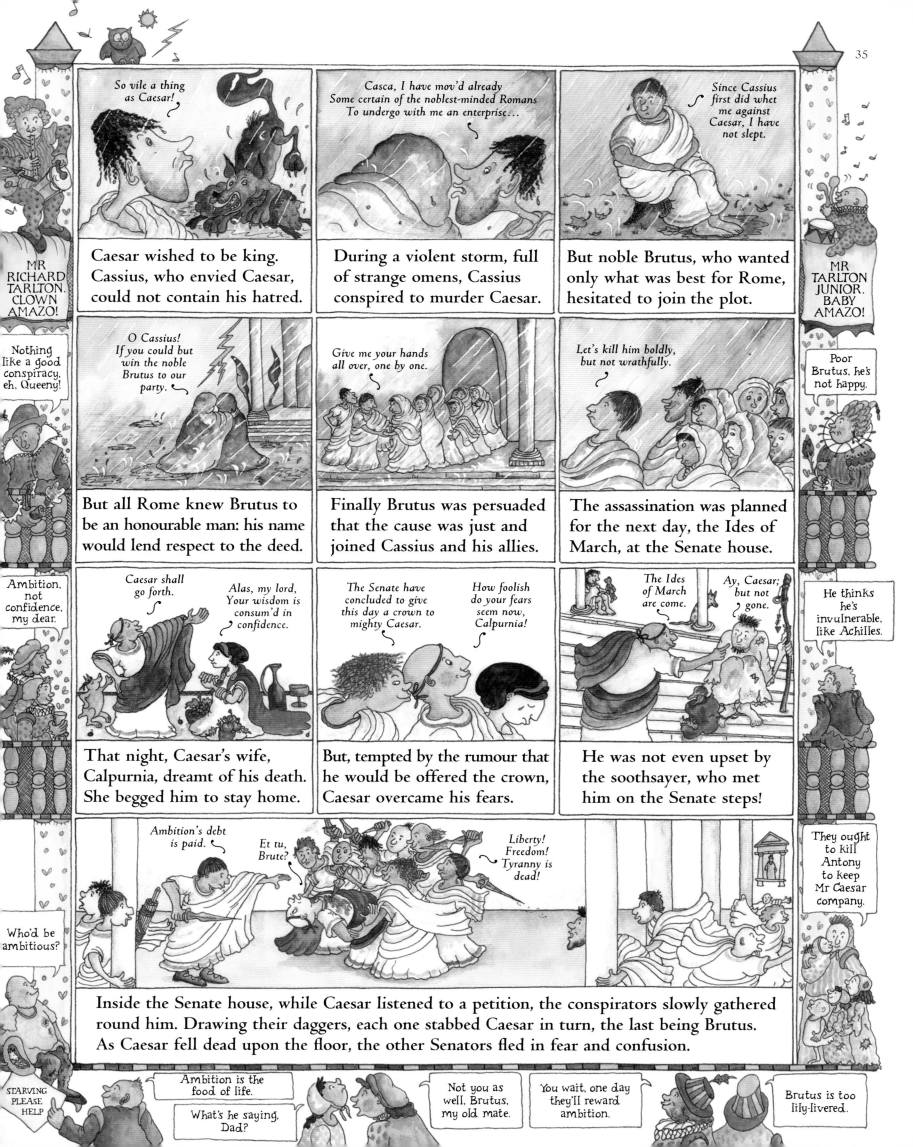

THE TEMPEST

Many years ago on a mystical isle, young Miranda and her loving father, Prospero, watched as a ship foundered in a fierce and terrible tempest. Prospero had been preparing for this moment for years, developing his magic powers from a rare book until he could control the elements. Miranda suspected that her father had caused the storm, but had no idea why such a gentle man should wish to harm anyone. So Prospero revealed how he and his daughter had been cast away on the island, twelve years before.

As the wise old bear once said, you're never too young for adventure.

We like this, already.

For then thou wast not out three years old.

Thy father was the Duke of Milan.

Me, poor man, my library was dukedom large enough.

My brother, and thy uncle, call'd Antonio...

did believe he was indeed the duke.

The king of Naples... hearkens my brother's suit.

They hurried us aboard a barque;

bore us some leagues to sea.

Some food we had, and some fresh water.

Here in this island we arrived.

Prospero had been Duke of Milan until his brother Antonio, aided by Alonso, King of Naples, seized power. Prospero and Miranda were set adrift in a tiny boat, but luckily a friend, Gonzalo, had secreted books and provisions on board. These sustained the pair until they drifted on to an island.

I bet he picks his nose.

When I was little sprites were two ducat!

The only inhabitants on this isle were the monster Caliban and the sprites his mother had trapped in trees before she died. Caliban became Prospero's servant, as did Ariel, an airy sprite. Ariel, who was invisible to all but Prospero, had been freed from a tree by Prospero's magic and in return had promised to serve him faithfully for twelve years.

Give us a posy.

Can you see Ariel?

No.

I think Ariel's hidden in the star.

You don't know nothing.

He's right.

Who's right?

I'm right. Ariel's just air.

Know-all.

By accident most strange, bountiful fortune, Now my dear lady, hath mine enemies Brought to this shore.

But are they, Ariel, safe?

Not a hair perish'd... The king's son have I landed by himself.

Prospero told Miranda that the storm-tossed ship carried his old enemies. Then, seeing Ariel approach, Prospero put a plan into action and sent Miranda to sleep.

Ariel spirited the ship's company ashore, isolating all but Antonio, Gonzalo and King Alonso. So the king feared that his son, Prince Ferdinand, must have drowned.

The thunder's over now, dearie.

Go, make thyself like to a nymph of the sea.

Hag-seed, hence! Fetch us in fuel.

I must obey: his art is of such power.

I might call him A thing divine.

O you wonder!

Full fathom five thy father lies.

Ariel, now in the guise of a sea nymph, went to fetch Ferdinand to Prospero's cave.

Having dispatched Caliban to gather wood, Prospero then woke Miranda.

Drawn to the cave by Ariel's singing, Ferdinand stared in wonder at lovely Miranda.

Potato?

...and hast put thyself upon this island as a spy.

No, as I am a man.

There's nothing ill can dwell in such a temple.

I'll manacle thy neck and feet together.

Beseech you, father!

A little adversity does wonders for love.

The two youngsters fell in love, as Prospero had planned. Adversity, he hoped, would seal the bond, so he accused Ferdinand of spying.

He forbade Miranda to talk to Ferdinand and sent him to shift logs, which Ferdinand did willingly, to stay close to his beloved.

Miranda, there are other men in the world.

I'll bear your logs the while.

No, precious creature.

Take my daughter.

For hours, Ferdinand hauled logs. Miranda never left his side.

Prospero watched Miranda and Ferdinand's love blossom, and finally he relented.

He conjured up a flock of nymphs to sing a blessing on their engagement.

It's a sprite.

Lo now! Lo! I'll fall flat.

Alas! The storm is come again.

This is some monster of the isle.

You're right there, you swiller!

PRIVATE BOX KEEP OUT

Meanwhile, Caliban gathered driftwood until a looming figure made him hide under his cloak.

It was Trinculo, King Alonso's jester who, fearing a storm, also crawled under the cloak.

Minutes later, Stefano, the king's drunken butler, fell over the heaving bundle.

ug!

If they've been shipwrecked, why aren't they wet?

It's magic, stupids.

I think I can see Ariel.

Only Prospero can.

Speech bubbles and captions:

O Stefano! — *Here, kiss the book.* — *Hast thou not dropped from heaven?*

Trinculo and Stefano were delighted to be reunited. Caliban, unaware of the shipwreck, thought they had dropped from the moon.

Thou shalt be lord of it and I'll serve thee. — *Monster, I will kill this man.*

Thinking they must be very powerful, Caliban urged the pair to assassinate Prospero. Ariel overheard and flew off to tell his master.

We must prepare to meet with Caliban. — *Ay, my commander.*

When the traitor Caliban drew near with his companions, Prospero was ready. Ariel had strewn Prospero's finest clothes before the cave.

O King Stefano! — *I'll have that gown.* — *Let it alone, thou fool.*

Caliban, Trinculo, and Stefano crept up, ready to kill Prospero, but were distracted by the array of handsome garments.

Hey, Mountain, hey! Fury, Fury! There tyrant . . . — *Silver! There it goes, Silver!*

When the murderous trio were half dressed, Prospero unleashed a pack of snarling phantom hounds. Driven by Ariel, the dogs chased the rascals far off across the island. Then Ariel returned to aid Prospero: the time had come for him to settle the score with his brother and King Alonso.

He is drowned whom thus we stray to find.

King Alonso, Antonio, and the good Gonzalo had been vainly searching for Ferdinand.

I will stand to and feed.

Tired and hungry, they were in despair, but then a table of food suddenly materialized.

You are three men of sin!

Amazed, they were about to eat when Ariel, disguised as a harpy, made the food vanish.

Him and his innocent child.

Ariel reminded them of their sins against Prospero. Guilt and fear froze their spirits.

Ariel drew them into a magic circle, where they were held like unwilling statues.

Behold, sir King, the wronged duke of Milan, Prospero.

Prospero, in his ducal robes, appeared before them as though risen from the dead.

Margin character speech bubbles (left):

Can I kiss the book?

I don't like not seeing Ariel.

Phantom, but fierce!

He's cuddling, not drowning.

Dad says my mum is a harpy.

Margin character speech bubbles (right):

Must be strong stuff!

If you wriggle, Caliban will get you.

Good doggies.

Tell me when it's over.

Could I be an extra if I were invisible?

Bottom margin speech bubbles:

If I looked like that I'd be invisible too.

Go and eat that fire somewhere else, we're concentrating.

Enjoying your outing, Grandpa?

You almost are, pal.

Antonio and King Alonso were awestruck into true repentance and begged to be forgiven. At last Prospero's anger was placated.

Prospero released them from the circle and led them, and his old friend Gonzalo, to where Ferdinand and Miranda sat playing chess.

King Alonso was overjoyed at finding his son alive and embraced him warmly. Ferdinand told the king of his wish to marry Miranda. Seeing Miranda's beauty and his son's happiness, King Alonso gave his consent. He hoped the union would heal the rift between Milan and Naples.

Into the midst of their rejoicing came Caliban, Trinculo, and Stefano, urged on by Ariel. Prospero forgave them too, in return for a little hard labor. The party then made themselves comfortable, while Prospero recounted his adventures of the past twelve years.

They all planned to sail to Naples the next morning for the wedding of Miranda and Ferdinand, after which Prospero would return to Milan as its rightful duke. That night, Prospero released his faithful Ariel, who promised him fair winds for their journey. Then Prospero discarded his magic cloak, buried his staff deep in the ground, and threw his book of magic out to sea. After twelve years, Prospero was leaving the enchanted island to Caliban and the sprites. Prospero's tempest had served its purpose, and his dukedom was restored.

AS YOU LIKE IT

Alas!

Many summers ago, in France, Duke Frederick's court was enjoying a day of wrestling. The fearsome giant, Monsieur Charles, was taking on all comers. Only Rosalind, Frederick's niece, was sad. She was pining for her father, the rightful duke, whom Frederick had banished to the Forest of Arden after stealing his crown.

I pray thee, Rosalind, sweet my coz, be merry.

Neither her dear cousin, Celia, nor Touchstone, the jester, could comfort Rosalind.

Give over this attempt.
Do, young sir.

And now Orlando, to whom Rosalind had taken a fancy, was going to fight Monsieur Charles.

The little strength that I have, I would it were with you.

Orlando had also fallen for Rosalind, so he wanted to prove his strength.

Yo! Yo! Orlando.

Orlando was strong indeed! Everyone watched in awe as he skilfully floored the giant.

I would thou hadst told me of another father.

Even Frederick cheered, until he learned Orlando's father had been his enemy.

I do in friendship counsel you to leave this place.
Wear this for me.

A courtier urged Orlando to leave court. Rosalind sadly gave her love a parting gift.

Ooh, Ducky it's love!

He's a real tyrant.

Mistress, dispatch you with your safest haste, And get you from our court.
If she be a traitor, why so am I.

But Frederick then threw Rosalind from court. Celia, his daughter, was shocked. She resolved to leave too, and help Rosalind find her father.

Call me Ganymede.
No longer Celia, but Aliena.

They decided to travel to the Forest of Arden in disguise, Rosalind as the poor youth, "Ganymede", and Celia as his sister, "Aliena".

They are brave going to the forest!
It's not scary.

Takes one to know one!
Ooh, the old imposter!
Throw a rat at him!
Want to buy an orange for the journey?
Don't be daft, they need ale!
Is the jes going to

Orlando returned to the home he shared with his older brother, Oliver. Adam, an elderly servant, greeted him with bad news.

Oliver, who had always been jealous of Orlando, planned to murder him. Orlando fled with Adam to the Forest of Arden.

When Duke Frederick heard that Orlando and Adam had fled to Arden too, he hoped they might lead him to his beloved daughter, Celia. He sent for Oliver and ordered him to go and look for Orlando in the forest.

In the meantime, "Ganymede", "Aliena" and their companion, Touchstone, had reached the forest. They felt exhausted and afraid.

A kind shepherd helped them find food and shelter, so they could rest before beginning their search for Rosalind's father.

When Orlando and Adam reached the forest, they too felt tired and hungry, especially the aged Adam. Fortunately, they came across the deposed duke's camp where they were made welcome. As Adam revived, one of the duke's courtiers, Jaques, entertained them with a long speech.

In the mysterious, magical Forest of Arden, strange things began to happen. Touchstone the jester fell for Audrey, a goatherd. Phebe, a shepherdess, fell for "Ganymede", making her sweetheart, Silvius, sad. Orlando professed his love for Rosalind to "Ganymede", who dared not reveal her disguise. Only "Aliena" was without an admirer.

Then one day in the forest, Orlando found a lion and a snake about to attack a sleeping man.

The snake vanished when it saw Orlando, but the lion prepared to pounce.

Orlando realized the man was Oliver, his brother. He slew the lion and saved him. Oliver felt ashamed and the brothers were reunited.

But Orlando was due to visit "Ganymede" and "Aliena". He sent Oliver ahead to explain the delay, while he bandaged a wound.

At first sight, Oliver and "Aliena" fell head over heels in love.

Oliver raced back to tell Orlando all about "Aliena".

Orlando, no stranger to instant love, bid him marry the next day.

At last, "Aliena" had found both love and a husband.

It was a lover and his lass,
With a hey, and a ho, and a hey nonino.

That o'er the green corn-field did pass,
In the spring time, the only pretty ring time,
When birds do sing, hey ding a ding, ding...

THE BLACK-FRIARS BOYS

I am a magician.

You will have her when I bring her? — That would I.

You will bestow Rosalind on Orlando? — That would I.

From hence I go.

Thanks to "Ganymede", the wedding did not go quite as expected.

First, she made Orlando vow to marry Rosalind if she could find her.

Then she made her father, the duke, vow to give Rosalind away.

Finally, "Ganymede" vanished with the bride, "Aliena".

I love a happy ending!

But what will happen when they leave the forest?

You're bloomin' gloom and doom.

Verily, a merry play!

Hey. Ding. Ding. Ding. Ding.

I love it when Will goes daft!

Can I touch the fairies? — No, they're moths!

What's a Greek god doing here?

Truly, it makes you want to dance!

When they reappeared, the girls were dressed once more as Rosalind and Celia. Hymen, the god of marriage, attended them. The duke was overjoyed, and Orlando and Oliver embraced their transformed lovers. When Phebe saw that "Ganymede" was a girl, she at last fell in love with Silvius. Touchstone and Audrey skipped with delight. In the midst of all this joy, a messenger came from Frederick to say he repented of his wicked ways and wished to return the crown to his brother, the rightful duke. After Hymen had blessed the happy couples, everyone sang and danced for one last day in the mysterious Forest of Arden.

A verily merrily play, I say!

Verily, verily, merrily, merrily...

Too good to be true, I say! — Don't be daft, it's a play.

Are you allowed? — Nay!

Get this ass out of here. — When are you leavin' then?

ANTONY AND CLEOPATRA

Three men, Mark Antony, young Octavius Caesar and Aemilius Lepidus once ruled the Roman world. Caesar and Lepidus took care of the affairs of state in Italy, but Antony made merry in Egypt.

Antony was in love with Egypt's queen, Cleopatra, and could not bear to leave her.

But news came that his wife, Fulvia, had died and his power in Rome was weakening.

In spite of Cleopatra's pleas, Antony and his good friend, Enobarbus, left for Rome.

Caesar and Lepidus resented the time the once noble Antony spent in Egypt, and despised his neglect of duty.

In order to strengthen his alliance with the two leaders once more, Antony agreed to marry Caesar's sister, Octavia.

Next, the three rulers set about retrieving their strength at sea, which another powerful Roman general, Sextus Pompey, had usurped during Antony's long absence. A peace treaty was signed and Antony celebrated late into the night with his old friend, Pompey.

Antony felt he had now done everything he could to retain his position. He left for Athens with Octavia.

But before long, news reached Athens that Caesar had killed Pompey, imprisoned Lepidus and publicly scorned Antony.

Only Octavia might be able to prevent a war between her husband and brother. She left for Rome at once.

Octavia chose to travel the distance without ceremony, but her modest arrival infuriated Caesar. He felt Antony had insulted his sister.

Then came the news that, in Octavia's absence, Antony had gone to see Cleopatra in Egypt. War between the two leaders was inevitable.

When Cleopatra had heard the news of Antony's marriage to Octavia she had nearly murdered the messenger in a jealous fury. But when Antony came back to her, she welcomed him with open arms.

The reunited lovers decided to fight Caesar at sea, their galleys sailing together.

Enobarbus begged Antony not to fight at sea. Antony was better at fighting on land.

But Antony had ears only for Cleopatra. They left for their ships, side by side.

Antony and Cleopatra's vessels sped swiftly across the Ionian Sea towards Caesar's fleet.

The lighter Roman ships darted amongst the Egyptian vessels. Arrows and spears speckled the air.

Then, suddenly, Cleopatra fled from the battle with all her ships.

All might have been well had Antony not followed her, leaving his own fleet without a leader.

O! Whither hast thou led me, Egypt?

I little thought you would have follow'd.

My heart was to thy rudder tied by the strings.

O! My pardon!

Pardon, pardon!

Fall not a tear, I say; one of them rates all that is won and lost. Give me a kiss.

Some of Antony's ships survived, but most were sunk by the Romans. Antony had sacrificed everything for love – his honour, his power and his men. He raged against the queen. He felt so ashamed, he contemplated death. But in the end, Cleopatra won his heart again.

WATER MUSIC EXTRA

Guess who can't swim!

Verily, Egypt's got windy.

Love before honour. Poor show.

YOUR COUNTRY NEEDS YOU!

Well, I blame this foreign travel lark.

Mmm, lark stew. Very nice.

FRESH FISH 1p!

If this sea isn't mopped up, I'm closing the theatre!

Master of the Revels ONLY

KEEP OUT!

RATS!

And that is the mighty Antony! Once the best soldier in the Roman world. Kissy! Kissy!

BOO!
BOO!
BOO!

Deaf as a pyramid.

Belt up and listen!

Lord of his fortunes he salutes thee… Let him breathe between the heavens and earth a private man in Athens; this for him. Next, Cleopatra does confess thy greatness, submits her to thy might.

For Antony, I have no ears for his request.

Antony and Cleopatra sent a messenger to Rome to offer Caesar terms for peace. But Caesar would not forgive Antony. And he sent word that he would make peace with Cleopatra only if she drove Antony from Egypt, or had him killed.

Yoohoo, handsome Thyreus! Over here!

Cleopatra's swallowed your sinews.

He knows that you embrace not Antony as you did love, but as you fear'd him.

Moon and stars! Whip him.

That's my brave lord!

I will be treble-sinew'd.

Caesar also sent a cunning soldier, Thyreus, to try to win Cleopatra from Antony.

When Antony saw Thyreus kiss Cleopatra's hand he suspected her of treachery.

Once more Cleopatra soothed Antony's anger. He decided to fight on against Caesar.

Yes, gone over to Caesar, and who can blame him?

That pig had sinews until you ate them!

Who's gone this morning?

Call for Enobarbus, he shall not hear thee.

O! My fortunes have corrupted honest men.

Run one before and let the Queen know.

Lord of lords!

My nightingale.

Much of Antony's army had deserted. Now Enobarbus left.

It was with a heavy heart that Antony went into battle.

Yet the victory that day went to him.

Cleopatra and Antony celebrated all through the night.

She's made a dolt of you.

All is lost! This foul Egyptian hath betrayed me. My fleet hath yielded to the foe.

The following day the battle moved from land to sea and Antony manned Cleopatra's galleys with his best troops. Once more, Antony seemed assured of victory. But then, without warning, Cleopatra's boats yielded again to Caesar.

She's a rum one, that Cleo.

You've got to be rum to build those pyramid things.

Chin up, pet, I loves yer.

Ho, ho! That'll really help.

The Tragedy of KING RICHARD III

Since I cannot prove a lover, to entertain these fair well-spoken days, I am determined to prove a villain.

In 1483, King Edward IV of England lay close to death. His son, the Prince of Wales, would inherit the crown even though he was still a child. The boy's uncle, hunchbacked Richard, Duke of Gloucester, had been made "Lord Protector" of the realm, and entrusted with the prince's care. But really Richard wanted the crown himself. And he was ready to use any means to get it, however foul…

I feel a bit of intrigue coming on.

Foul devil. / *Lady, you know no rules of charity.*

Out of my sight! Thou dost infect mine eyes. / *Thine eyes, sweet lady, have infected mine.*

Though I wish thy death, I will not be thy executioner. / *Vouchsafe to wear this ring.*

How does he get away with it?

Richard knew a king should have a well-born wife. He decided to court Anne, a royal widow. Since Richard himself had killed her husband and her father-in-law, Anne was disgusted when he came to woo her at the funeral. But the wily Richard talked so cleverly he won her round.

Family loyalty! I love it.

His majesty … hath appointed This conduct to convey me to the Tower. / *I will deliver you.*

Who'd kill for a crown?

Richard also needed to be rid of his older brother, the popular Duke of Clarence. He persuaded the weakening King Edward to imprison him as a traitor in the terrible Tower of London. The unsuspecting Clarence loved Richard and trusted him to secure his release.

Elizabeth E·R.

Shall we stab him as he sleeps? / *No; he'll say 'twas done cowardly, when he wakes.*

I will send you to my brother Gloucester. / *Your brother Gloucester hates you.*

Relent and save your souls. / *Relent! 'Tis cowardly.*

If all this will not do, I'll drown you in the malmsey-butt within.

Not in my butt you don't!

Instead, Richard hired a pair of assassins to murder Clarence in his cell.

BEWARE! PICKPOCKETS OPERATE IN THIS AREA

Verily, 'tis hard to believe such wickedness. / *Methinks Richard's pockets would be rich pickings.* / *Rich in evil!* / *Aah, "To sleep: perchance to dream…" Now who said that?*

Madam, bethink you, like a careful mother, of the young prince your son: send straight for him; let him be crown'd.

My other self … my oracle, my prophet!

My lord … let not us two stay at home.

Soon King Edward died. His widow, Queen Elizabeth – well aware of Richard's ambition – quickly sent her brothers to bring the Prince of Wales back to London for his coronation.

But Richard and his sly friend, the Duke of Buckingham, pursued them.

Sanctuary won't save you. Flee the country.

Come, come, my boy; we will to sanctuary.

I'll conduct you to the sanctuary.

I shall not sleep in quiet at the Tower.

I fear no Uncles dead.

Nor none that live, I hope.

You'll sleep quiet. He'll see to that.

When Elizabeth heard Richard had taken her eldest son and imprisoned her brothers, she was scared. She fled with her second son, the young Duke of York, and sought holy sanctuary.

But Richard had no respect for holy sanctuary, and ordered little York to be taken from his mother. Then he locked the two young princes in the Tower, safely out of the way.

Unwise words, sirrah!

I'll have this crown of mine cut from my shoulders Before I'll see the crown so foul misplac'd.

Look how I am bewitch'd; behold mine arm…

Thou protector of this damned strumpet!

Off with his head!

O bloody Richard! Miserable England!

Chip-chop! Many a true word…

By now Hastings, the Lord Chamberlain, had guessed Richard's plans.

So Richard falsely accused Queen Elizabeth of witchcraft.

He knew Hastings would never sign her death warrant.

He then declared Hastings a traitor and had him beheaded.

I warrant they won't be joyful for long!

Good my lord; your citizens entreat you.

Refuse not, mighty, lord.

O! Make them joyful.

Ha! Am I king? 'Tis so: but… I wish the bastards dead.

Could he kill the little princes?

Next, Buckingham spread rumours that the royal princes had been born out of wedlock. Soon the people began to call for Richard to be king.

The villain had succeeded! He was crowned King Richard III of England. But he did not feel safe while the little princes still lived.

Break out the rotten eggs!

But don't hit Hastings.

Give us some.

So the killing doesn't end here?

Now, do you dare turn the page?

But his friend Buckingham was reluctant to kill the children.

So Richard paid an assassin to smother the boys as they slept.

Angry with Buckingham, Richard refused him a long-promised earldom.

Buckingham fled to join the growing forces against the king.

Richard believed he could be secure only if he got rid of Anne and married the dead princes' sister, Elizabeth. But news came that Henry, Earl of Richmond, was marching against him.

Richard knew he must fight Richmond or lose the crown. He rallied his army and set out for Wales. Along the way he was delighted to hear that his men had captured Buckingham.

The armies met on Bosworth Field. The night before battle began, both the king and Richmond dreamed of Richard's victims. One by one, the spectres wished Richard ill and the earl well.

A horse! A horse! My kingdom for a horse!

Good old Will! He never stints on blood and gore.

1564

I auditioned to be a soldier but, "No, not today, thanks..."

NO MUSIC WILL BE PLAYED IN THE BATTLE SCENE

Bleeding bodies everywhere. I'll close this theatre down!

Master of the Revels ONLY

Blackfriars only 1p! Avoid the bridge! Avoid the crowds! Avoid your neighbours! Take the ferry! Boat leaves in ten minutes!

The day dawned sunless and cold. Soon the field was loud with the noise of battle. Richard's side suffered heavy losses. Then his own horse was slain beneath him. But he fought on bravely until he met Richmond. The raging hunchback was no match for the earl. With one victorious stroke Richmond slew him. Richard III's short and bloody reign was over. Few mourned its passing and many celebrated the crowning of Richmond as King Henry VII. Henry then married the princes' sister, Elizabeth – uniting her house, of York, and his, of Lancaster, to bring peace to England.

Well you look dead already.

You'd have to be brain dead to fight for Richard.

Being a groundling is a pain in the neck!

Your grandfather fought at the battle of Bosworth.

Was he an actor then?

TWELFTH NIGHT;
or, What You Will

On a stormy night off the rocky coast of Illyria, a ship was wrecked. One of the few survivors was a gentlewoman named Viola. Her beloved twin brother, Sebastian, had vanished in the waves and Viola feared he was drowned. The ship's captain advised Viola to dress as a man and seek work at the court of Illyria's ruler, Duke Orsino.

His eyes must be blinded by tears.

I have unclasp'd to thee the book even of my secret soul.

Duke Orsino employed Viola as his page. Soon he came to trust her above all others.

Unfold the passion of my love.

I'll do my best to woo your lady.

You've left out, "If music be the food of love, play on."

BOOK HOLDER'S BOX NO ENTRY SILENCE

He told her that he loved a countess called Olivia, and asked her to deliver messages of love. Viola did not relish the task for she had fallen in love with Orsino herself. But she agreed to go.

Is all Illyria blind?

Madam, yond young fellow swears he will speak with you.

I told him you were sick.

I told him you were asleep.

Let him approach.

I cannot love him.

Methinks she's smitten by the page!

Olivia was in mourning for her dead brother and allowed no men into her house. But Orsino's page would not be turned away, even by Olivia's rude steward, Malvolio.

Olivia explained to Viola that she did not love his master and never would.

Verily, I think they are all blind.

How now! Even so quickly may one catch the plague?

Hie thee, Malvolio.

Poor lady, she were better love a dream.

"But love is blind, and lovers cannot see..."

But Orsino's page talked so eloquently of love that Olivia began to fall in love with *him!*

When Viola left, Olivia sent Malvolio after the handsome page with a ring.

Realizing what must have happened, Viola wished she could reveal her disguise.

If she finds out now, there's no plot.

A plague o' these pickled herring.

How now, sot.

Swabber!

Another eternal truth, my sweet Will.

Did I not say that?

That night, Olivia went to bed. But her maid, Maria; her jester, Feste; her uncle, Sir Toby Belch and his friend, Sir Andrew Aguecheek (who Sir Toby hoped might marry Olivia), stayed up late, revelling and drinking. Suddenly, Malvolio burst in and rudely packed them off to bed.

Next day, the angry revellers decided to pay Malvolio back. They dropped a letter in his path, written by Maria in Olivia's handwriting. If Malvolio would only smile and wear yellow, cross-gartered stockings, the letter said, Olivia might marry him.

Of course, when Malvolio did smile and strut his yellow stockings at her, Olivia thought he had gone mad. He quoted whole sentences from the letter, but still she looked bewildered. Finally, she gave orders that he be locked up in a dark room till he recovered.

Later Viola arrived. She was still acting as Orsino's page.

Again Olivia rejected Orsino. She wanted to wed his page.

Olivia begged the horrified page not to leave her.

Sir Andrew angrily decided to challenge this new rival to a duel.

Meanwhile, Antonio, an old enemy of Orsino's, had saved Sebastian, Viola's twin. Antonio lent Sebastian his purse and went looking for lodgings.

But half an hour later Antonio saw Sebastian again. In fact it was Viola, duelling with Sir Andrew. Antonio rushed to "Sebastian's" defence.

Unluckily, some soldiers recognized Antonio as the duke's enemy and arrested him.

Antonio asked "Sebastian" to buy his freedom. But Viola was astonished and refused.

Then she guessed that this man must know her brother. He must still be alive!

But Sir Andrew still wanted his duel. He and Toby chased Viola, and caught – Sebastian.

Luckily, Olivia came by. Mistaking Sebastian for Viola as well, she rescued him.

While he was still in a daze, Olivia rushed Sebastian off to be married.

Afterwards, the confused but happy Sebastian insisted on leaving his new bride while he returned Antonio's purse.

At the same time, Duke Orsino (who knew nothing of the wedding) set out with Viola to woo Countess Olivia once more.

On their way, they met Antonio, who complained that the duke's page had his purse. Then up hobbled Sir Toby and Sir Andrew complaining that the duke's page had wounded them. Then, to both the duke's and Viola's horror, Olivia arrived greeting Viola as "husband"!

Then, suddenly, another Viola appeared. It seemed the page had a twin brother.

As Viola embraced Sebastian and explained she was his sister, the confusion cleared...

Duke Orsino was so amazed, he gave up his wasted love for Olivia and offered his heart to Viola, the woman who had been his page. Antonio was pardoned and got his purse back. And Olivia and Sebastian were happily reunited. As Olivia's jester, Feste, began to sing a song of celebration, everyone, except the yellow-stockinged Malvolio, linked arms in love and friendship. The terrible shipwreck on Illyria's shores had turned out to be a stroke of great good fortune.

KING LEAR

Which of you shall we say doth love us most?

In ancient Britain, the elderly King Lear decided to give up his power and divide his kingdom among his three daughters. He planned to give the largest territory to the daughter who professed to love him most. Lear was sure this would be his favourite, Cordelia.

Sir, I love you more than words can wield the matter.

The eldest, greedy Goneril of Albany, pretended to love her father very much.

She comes too short.

Lear's second daughter, Regan of Cornwall, swore she loved him even more than Goneril.

I love your majesty according to my bond; nor more nor less.

So young, and so untender?

But Cordelia, sickened by their deceit, said only that she loved him as a daughter should.

Thy truth then be thy dower.

At this, Lear flew into a rage. He disowned Cordelia and gave his lands to Goneril and Regan.

Check this hideous rashness.

Away!

When Lear's oldest friend, the Earl of Kent, tried to intervene, Lear banished him on the spot.

Thee and thy virtues here I seize upon.

But Cordelia's suitor, the King of France, admired her honesty, and asked her to marry him.

The jewels of our father, with wash'd eyes Cordelia leaves you.

Cordelia prepared to sail for France, reluctantly leaving her father in the care of her cunning sisters, Goneril and Regan.

Service.

But Kent did not leave. He disguised himself and took a job as Lear's servant, hoping to protect him from his scheming daughters.

Lear had no palace of his own now, so he took a train of one hundred knights, his fool and his new servant to stay with Goneril. But Goneril had changed. She was no longer a loving daughter.

Bewildered by her harshness, Lear decided to visit Regan. He sent his servant ahead to the Earl of Gloucester's palace where she and her husband were staying. He, his knights and his fool, followed, galloping through the night.

But when they arrived, Lear was outraged to discover that Regan and Cornwall had put his servant in the stocks. Nor would they come out and greet the king.

Then Goneril arrived, and the spiteful sisters told Lear he must give up his hundred knights and live as a pauper.

Lear had no daughters left to turn to. His heart bursting with sorrow, he rushed out on to the heath in a pitiless storm.

The Earl of Gloucester sadly watched Lear go. He too had suffered at the hands of his children. His youngest son, Edmund, had told him that Edgar, his favourite son, planned to murder him. This was a lie, but Gloucester had believed it and had driven Edgar out. He did not know that Edgar was living nearby in a hovel on the heath, disguised as a mad beggar.

It was into this hovel that Kent and the fool managed to drag King Lear for shelter. Edgar cowered in the shadows, delirious with cold.

Back at the palace, Gloucester overheard Regan and Goneril plotting to kill King Lear. He rushed out at once to warn Kent.

But on his return, Gloucester paid dearly for this act of loyalty.

Cornwall brutally tore out one of the old man's eyes.

A shocked servant tried to intervene, wounding Cornwall.

Urged on by Regan, Cornwall took out Gloucester's other eye.

But Cornwall's wound proved fatal. Regan was delighted. Now she would be free to marry Gloucester's son, Edmund, whom she loved.

But Goneril loved him too. Jealous of Regan, she wrote to Edmund suggesting he kill her husband, Albany, leaving *her* free to marry him.

But then news came that Cordelia had raised a French army and landed at Dover. Reluctantly the two sisters put their battle for Edmund to one side and prepared to fight Cordelia. They marshalled their troops and set off for Dover with Albany and Edmund.

Kent had also heard the news, and set out with Lear, hoping to reunite him with Cordelia. Blind Gloucester was on his way to Dover too with Edgar who had found him lost and in pain on the heath. Outside the port the two old men met: Gloucester now eyeless, and Lear mad with misery and fatigue. As the war drums rolled, Cordelia's servants came to take Lear to the French camp.

Take them away.

Come, let's away to prison. We two alone will sing like birds i' the cage.

King Lear slept through the long battle. When he awoke, Cordelia and the French had been defeated. Unaware that Edmund had issued orders for his and Cordelia's deaths, Lear rejoiced. The idea of imprisonment with Cordelia seemed like heaven compared to freedom with Goneril and Regan.

All this excitement is making me hungry.

Edmund, I arrest thee on capital treason.

Draw thy sword.

I should ask thy name.

Regan's looking a little quea[...]

Meanwhile, Albany had discovered Goneril and Edmund's plan to kill him. He declared Edmund a traitor and ordered him to defend himself.

An armoured man challenged Edmund to fight. Goneril and Regan watched as Edmund rapidly began to lose to the stranger.

Forsooth, dead bodies on stage are a health hazard!

My name is Edgar, and thy father's son.

But his flaw'd heart – Alack! Too weak the conflict to support.

This speech of yours hath mov'd me.

One thing's fo[...] sure, thi[...] will not e[...] happily.

Master of the Revels ONLY

Only after he had delivered a mortal blow to Edmund, did the stranger remove his helmet and reveal himself to be Edgar.

As Edmund lay dying, Edgar told him how he had been reunited with their father, Gloucester, just before his recent death.

Who dead?

Your lady, sir, your lady: and her sister.

I was contracted to them both.

My writ is on the life of Lear and on Cordelia. Nay, send in time.

Run, run! O run!

Oh, hurr[...] Save the[...] save ther[...]

Miaow!

A servant brought news that Goneril had poisoned Regan and then, realizing Edmund would not live, had killed herself too.

Edmund was conscience-stricken at last. With his final breath he told Edgar to send a reprieve for Lear and Cordelia.

Woof!

Eeek!

Hey! I told you before, them's my apples.

Brother killing brother and sister killing sister...

And all in the same scene.

Shall we leave? It's too sad.

Howl, howl, howl, howl!
O! You are men of stones:
Had I your tongues and eyes,
I'd use them so that heaven's
vaults should crack.

But it was too late. Lear's dear Cordelia had been hanged. Albany and Edgar watched in horror as Lear stumbled towards them carrying her body in his arms.

The weight of this sad time
we must obey;
Speak what we feel, not what
we ought to say.

Beside himself with grief, the old king fell into a faint. Edgar tried to help, but Kent stopped him. Lear had lost everything. What he had not given away had been taken from him. Even his fool had been executed. Kent, who had stayed by the king's side throughout his torments, knew Lear no longer had any hope of finding peace in this world. It was with relief that he watched his friend's life gently ebb from him, his arms about his only true daughter, Cordelia. Albany tried to persuade Kent to take the crown, but the old earl had no use for life without Lear. So Edgar became king and tried to rule with honour, in memory of two wronged old men: his father, the Earl of Gloucester, and his liege, King Lear.

This play will certainly keep the gravedigger in work.

Shall I be queen now?

Wise words, but a bit late.

Wise words always come too bloomin' late.

Kent for King!

No, he's after following Lear.

The wife's pies for sale, or even the wife.

Watch it, you!

You won't treat your old Dad like that?

A pox on all this sadness. Let's see if the Rose has a merrier play.

The Merchant of Venice

Bassanio, a poor nobleman from Venice, was in love with Portia, a rich heiress from the country. To travel to her estate and court her, he needed three thousand ducats. His friend, the merchant Antonio, could not help. His wealth was with his ships at sea. So they asked the Jewish money-lender, Shylock. Shylock had long hated Antonio. He agreed to lend the sum, on one condition.

If the money was not returned in three months, Antonio must pay with a pound of his flesh. Antonio rashly agreed.

Bassanio now prepared to woo Portia at her house in Belmont. His good friend, Gratiano, begged to accompany him.

Before he died, Portia's father had made three caskets – one gold, one silver, one lead. On each was a riddle. The first suitor to pick the casket that contained a portrait of his daughter would win her hand. Men had flocked from far and near to try the test. All had failed.

1595

Young, learned and in disguise. Nod, nod, wink, wink.

Elizabeth E. R.

Verily, I'll not watch flesh-cutting!

She will!

STICK NO BILLS

Is this really a comedy?

BUY YOUR BUNS IN PUDDING LANE BAKERY

Call yourself Christian?

How shalt thou hope for mercy, rendering none?

What judgment shall I dread, doing no wrong?

In Venice, the duke and his nobles were in court. Shylock refused to take the larger sum Bassanio offered. He wanted his pound of flesh. So the duke sent for an expert, Doctor Bellario, for advice. The learned doctor was unwell, but sent in his place a promising pupil and his clerk.

Do you confess the bond? — *I do.*

The young lawyer confirmed the law stood against Antonio.

Why dost thou whet thy knife? — *To cut the forfeiture.*

Shylock was delighted and began to sharpen his knife.

The quality of mercy is not strain'd, It droppeth as the gentle rain from heaven...

The lawyer asked Shylock to be merciful and drop the charge.

I crave the law.

Shylock would not. He wished revenge upon his old enemy.

I am arm'd and well prepar'd.

Shylock steadied his knife and Antonio prepared to die.

Nor cut thou less, nor more, but just a pound of flesh.

The lawyer warned Shylock to take a pound of flesh *exactly*.

Shed thou no blood.

If he spilled one drop of blood, he would break the law.

Let the Christian go.

Shylock dropped his knife. He would take the money.

Therefore thou must be hang'd at the state's charge.

But the lawyer had more to say. Shylock had sought the life of a citizen of Venice. The punishment was death, if the duke decreed it.

I pardon thee thy life before thou ask it. — *I am not well.*

But the duke said that if Shylock became a Christian, he could keep his life. If he left his wealth to Jessica, he could keep his trade.

Go, Gratiano; run and overtake him; give him the ring.

The lawyer had saved Antonio's life. Yet he wanted no fee – only Bassanio's ring. Bassanio refused. Antonio begged his friend to reconsider.

My Lord Bassanio upon more advice Hath sent you here this ring. — *I'll see if I can get my husband's ring...*

Gratiano went after the lawyer with the ring. The clerk persuaded him to part with his ring too. Now what would the men tell their wives?

Don't look at me, my flesh's taken

The scales of justice are tipping!

Lend us a ducat or two, Shylock

You boys are in trouble now

Well, I feel sorry for Shylock.

He was only doing his job.

It's a fleshy plot!

A golden play.

Sparkles like silver.

Dull as lead.

Tell me where is fancy bred,
Or in the heart or in the head?
How begot, how nourished?

It is engender'd in the eyes,
With gazing fed; and fancy dies.

67

If you do love me, you will find me out.

Thou gaudy gold ... I will none of thee.

Ding, dong, bell.

ONE DAY ONLY! DON PEDRO FROM VENICE

ONE SEASON ONLY! DON JOHN FROM LUDGATE

Now Bassanio took his turn. Portia, who loved Bassanio as much as he loved her, watched nervously, with Nerissa, her maid, and Gratiano. Gold? Silver? Or lead? Which would Bassanio choose? At last, he turned the key in the lead casket ... and found his true love's portrait!

I think he's just a fortune-hunter.

No, he really loves her.

Bad news always comes in from the outside...

Have you been eating too many nuts?

But who comes here?

Portia gave Bassanio a ring. He swore never to part with it.

Then Nerissa gave Gratiano a ring. They had also found love.

Amid this joy, Bassanio's friend, Lorenzo, arrived. He had eloped with Shylock's daughter, Jessica. They brought grave news from Venice.

Really loves her money, d'you mean?

I hear Will borrowed from a lender to build this place.

It will go hard with poor Antonio.

You shall have gold to pay the petty debt twenty times over.

I will make haste.

Antonio's ships had not docked and the three months were up. Shylock was demanding his bond. Antonio's life was in danger.

The couples married in haste. Then Bassanio and Gratiano left for Venice. Portia promised enough money to pay off the debt many times over.

Can't you keep those mutts under control?

Well he certainly didn't borrow to give to me.

See thou render this Into my cousin's hand.

Madam, I go with all convenient speed.

We'll see our husbands Before they think of us.

ALMS

Left behind, Portia wrote to her cousin, a learned lawyer, Doctor Bellario. She asked him to send lawyers' clothes and books about the law.

Next Portia asked Lorenzo and Jessica to look after her house. She and Nerissa would await their husbands' return in a monastery.

A plague on all this kissing!

Oh go on! You love it really.

Portia's up to something.

But what?

Cease thy jabbering and you might find out.

How can I when groundlings pay only 1p for my genius!

In Venice, the duke and his nobles were in court. Shylock refused to take the larger sum Bassanio offered. He wanted his pound of flesh. So the duke sent for an expert, Doctor Bellario, for advice. The learned doctor was unwell, but sent in his place a promising pupil and his clerk.

The young lawyer confirmed the law stood against Antonio.

Shylock was delighted and began to sharpen his knife.

The lawyer asked Shylock to be merciful and drop the charge.

Shylock would not. He wished revenge upon his old enemy.

Shylock steadied his knife and Antonio prepared to die.

The lawyer warned Shylock to take a pound of flesh *exactly*.

If he spilled one drop of blood, he would break the law.

Shylock dropped his knife. He would take the money.

But the lawyer had more to say. Shylock had sought the life of a citizen of Venice. The punishment was death, if the duke decreed it.

But the duke said that if Shylock became a Christian, he could keep his life. If he left his wealth to Jessica, he could keep his trade.

The lawyer had saved Antonio's life. Yet he wanted no fee – only Bassanio's ring. Bassanio refused. Antonio begged his friend to reconsider.

Gratiano went after the lawyer with the ring. The clerk persuaded him to part with his ring too. Now what would the men tell their wives?

When Bassanio, Gratiano and Antonio reached Belmont, they never guessed Portia and Nerissa had just returned too.

At first the wives seemed pleased to see their husbands. Then Nerissa asked Gratiano where the ring she had given him was.

Soon Bassanio was in trouble with Portia too. Both wives claimed to be offended.

But when Antonio interceded, Portia relented. She bade him pass Bassanio a ring.

Nerissa also relented and gave Gratiano a ring. It seemed familiar.

Bassanio and Gratiano realized that these were the very rings they had given away. So Portia had been the young lawyer who had saved Antonio's life, and Nerissa her clerk! How blind they had been. Then Nerissa told Jessica that even though she had eloped with Lorenzo, she would inherit Shylock's wealth when he died. And Antonio discovered that his ships with all their merchandise had finally come safely into harbour. At last the merry friends could celebrate, and laugh at the husbands who had not known their own wives!

MUCH ADO ABOUT NOTHING

In Messina, Sicily, Governor Leonato's household was expecting guests – Don Pedro, the Prince of Aragon, his brother Don John, and two young officers, Claudio and Signior Benedick. The last time these gallants visited, they had been off to war. Now, they would have time for fun.

On their arrival, young Claudio realized he loved Leonato's daughter, sweet Hero. He asked the governor for her hand in marriage.

But when proud Signior Benedick met Hero's haughty cousin Beatrice once more, they fell to their old game of arguing.

Beatrice and Benedick both scorned the idea of marriage as much as they scorned one another. Each was determined to stay single.

But the prince, Don Pedro, thought they were well-matched. He asked Leonato, Claudio and Hero to help him trick them into marriage.

The next day Benedick just happened to overhear Don Pedro, Claudio and Leonato say that Beatrice was sick for love of him.

Convinced Leonato would not lie, Benedick believed them. He resolved to give up being proud and love Beatrice back.

Later, Beatrice just happened to overhear Hero and her maid say that Benedick was sick for love of her.

Convinced her sweet cousin would not lie, Beatrice believed them. She resolved to give up being haughty and return Benedick's love.

But meanwhile, Don Pedro's spiteful brother, Don John, and his cohort, Borachio, were plotting to ruin Hero's wedding plans.

Don John took Don Pedro and Claudio to a window, where they *thought* they saw Hero embrace Borachio.

The following day, as Friar Francis was about to marry them, Claudio accused Hero of disloyalty.

When Don Pedro also bore witness against Hero, even her own father began to believe the slanderous accusation.

However, Leonato soon came to his senses when Hero fell to the ground in a death-like trance. This also gave Friar Francis an idea.

He would take Hero into hiding and then announce the false news of her death. The shock might knock some sense into Claudio.

The first mask revealed Hero, not her unknown cousin. Claudio was overcome with joy!

The second hid Beatrice, still bent on teasing her beloved Benedick.

After much playful banter, which Benedick put a stop to with a kiss, Beatrice agreed to marry him. The delighted Friar Francis united the two couples. When news arrived that Don John had been captured, the wedding party decided to think about a punishment for him another day. Today was a day to revel in their recovered happiness, to feast and dance through the sun-filled day and sweet-scented Sicilian night!

William Shakespeare is one of the greatest writers of all time. Born in 1564, he wrote 38 plays and over 100 poems before his death at the age of 52 in 1616. Born and raised in Stratford-upon-Avon, the young Shakespeare started his career as an actor and a writer for the London stage, finding fame at the magnificent Globe Theatre. Little is known about the great bard himself, but his comedies, histories and tragedies have endured far beyond his own lifetime and are even more popular now than when they were first written.

Marcia Williams' mother was a novelist and her father a playwright, so it's not surprising that Marcia ended up an author herself. Her distinctive comic-strip style goes back to her schooldays in Sussex and the illustrated letters she sent home to her parents overseas. Although she never trained formally as an artist, she found that motherhood, and the time she spent later as a nursery school teacher, inspired her to start writing and illustrating children's books. Marcia's books bring to life some of the world's all-time favourite stories and some colourful historical characters. Her hilarious retellings and clever observations will have children laughing out loud and coming back for more!

More marvellous stories from
Marcia Williams

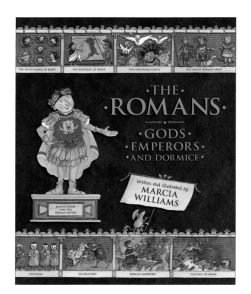

ISBN 978-1-4063-5455-3

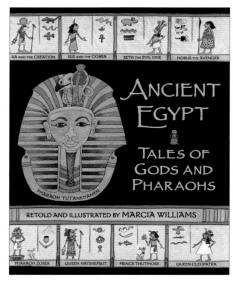

ISBN 978-1-4063-3832-4

ISBN 978-1-4063-4492-9

ISBN 978-1-4063-0347-6

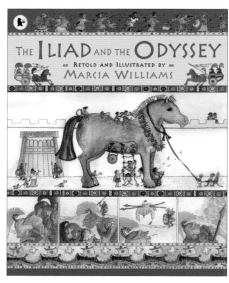

ISBN 978-1-4063-0348-3

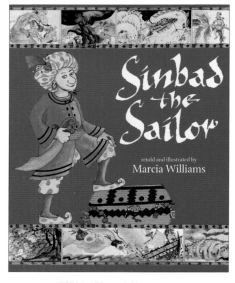

ISBN 978-1-4063-1944-6

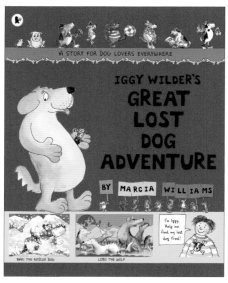

ISBN 978-1-4063-2997-1

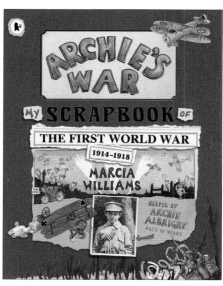

ISBN 978-1-4063-5268-9

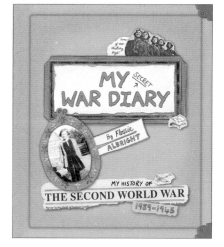

ISBN 978-1-4063-0940-9

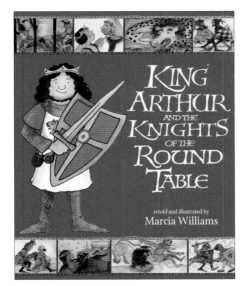

ISBN 978-1-4063-1866-1

ISBN 978-1-4063-0563-0

ISBN 978-1-4063-2610-9

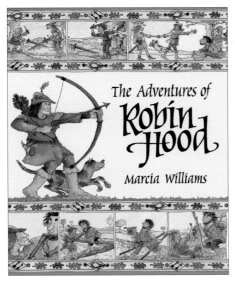

ISBN 978-1-4063-1137-2

ISBN 978-1-4063-0562-3

ISBN 978-1-4063-0171-7

ISBN 978-1-4063-4694-7

Available from
all good
booksellers

www.walker.co.uk

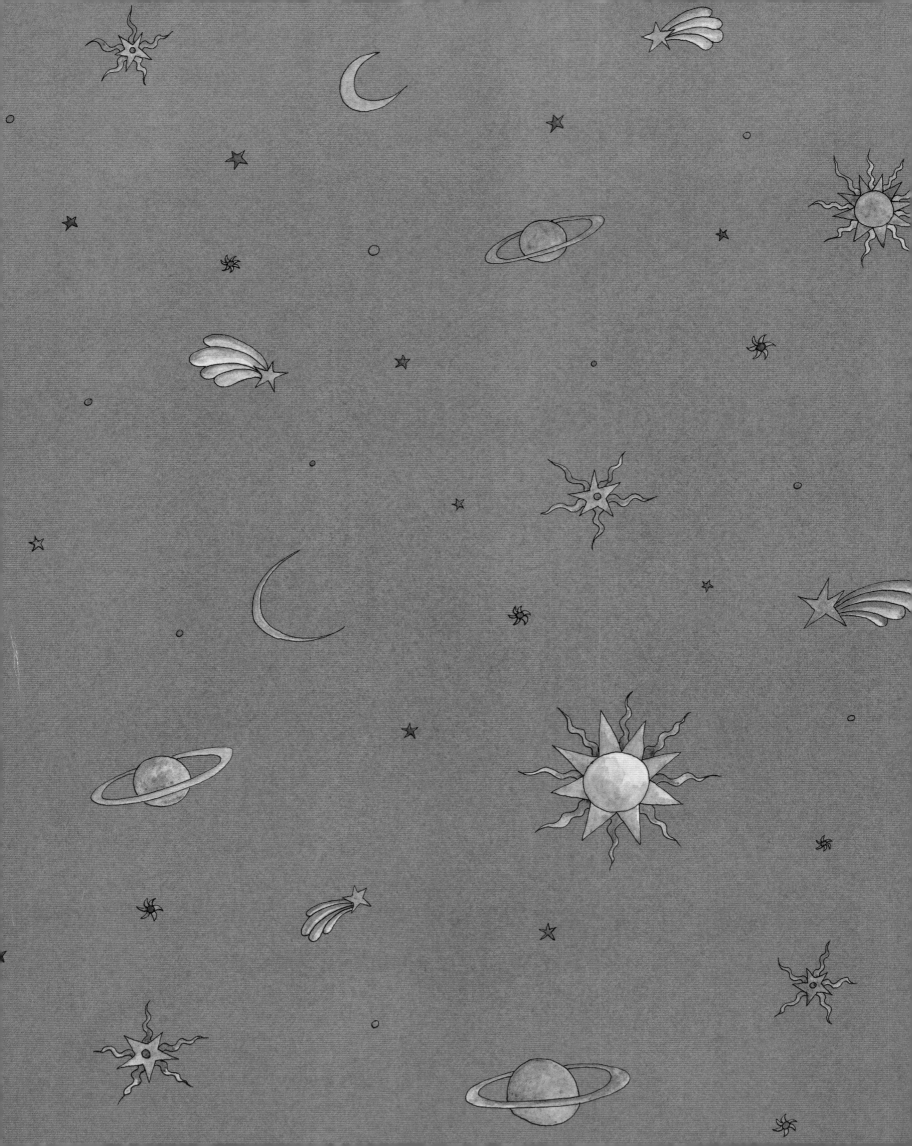